Consolidated B-36

By David Doyle

CW00763268

Published by
Ampersand Group, Inc.
A HobbyLink Japan company
235 NE 6th Ave., Suite B
Delray Beach, FL 33483-5543
561-266-9686 • 561-266-9786 Fax
www.ampersandpubco.com • www.hlj.com

Acknowledgments

It is not reasonably possible for one person to create a book on a historic subject such as theses Flying Wings. Rather, it requires what is in essence a team effort, with friends and colleagues each contributing. This book would not have been possible without such help—in essence collaboration—provided by Tom Kailbourn, Scott Taylor, Stan Piet, Brett Stolle at the National Museum of the United States Air Force, and the staffs of the National Archives, the San Diego Air and Space Museum and the American Aviation Historical Society. Of course, no one could ask for a better partner than I have in my wife Denise, whose ongoing support and help make these books possible.

Sources

AN 01-5EUC-2 "Erection and Maintenance Instructions, USAF Series B-36D Aircraft," Department of the Air Force, 3 June 1954.

TO 1B-36D(II)-1 "Flight Handbook USAF Series B-36D-II aircraft," Department of the Air Force, 18 May 1956.

AN 01-5EUG-1 "Flight Handbook USAF Series B-36H aircraft," Department of the Air Force, 13 November 1953.

TO 1B-36H(III)-1 "Flight Handbook USAF Series B-36H-III aircraft," Department of the Air Force, 24 November 1954.

AN 01-5EUJ-1 "Flight Handbook USAF Series B-36J aircraft," Department of the Air Force, 11 September 1953.

Pyeatt, Don and Jenkins, Dennis, "Cold War Peacemaker – the Story of Cowtown and the Convair B-36," Specialty Press, North Branch, MN, 2010

Jenkins, Dennis, "Magnesium Overcast – The Story of the Convair B-36," Specialty Press, North Branch, MN, 2001

Jacobsen, Meyers, "Convair B-36 Peacemaker," Schiffer Military History, Atglen, PA, 1999

Jacobsen, Meyers and Wagner, Ray, "B-36 In Action," Squadron/Signal Publications, Carrollton, TX, 1980

Front cover: Often referred to as the "Peacemaker," but never officially having been named such, the Convair B-36 was the biggest bomber aircraft ever flown by the United States Air Force. (Stan Piet collection)

Title page: The B-36 indeed reigned supreme among heavy bombers during the early days of the Cold War. With the longest wingspan of any combat aircraft ever built (at 230 feet it was 7 feet wider than even a C-5 Galaxy transport), and capable of carrying 86,000 pounds of bombs, the B-36 was the largest mass-produced piston-engined aircraft. (NARA)

Rear cover: B-36 bombers from the B-36D onward were powered by six Pratt and Whitney R-4360 Wasp Major engines as well as four General Electric J-47 turbojets, leading to the adage that the aircraft when operating properly "had six turning and four burning." The B-36 was America's front-line nuclear deterrent from 1948 until 12 February 1959, when the last B-36 was retired. (NARA)

Table of Contents

In the race to develop and deploy an intercontinental heavy bomber, the U.S. Army Air Forces considered the XB-35, a flying-wing aircraft produced by Northrop. The aircraft suffered stability problems, and the Air Force cancelled the flying-wing program in 1951. (National Museum of the United States Air Force)

The Consolidated B-36

Conceived during WWII, and first flown on 8 August 1946, seven decades later the Convair B-36 remains the largest bomber in the world. Although Convair, its manufacturer, pushed for the name "Peacemaker," the Air Force never adopted that, or any other, official name for the aircraft, unlike its contemporaries.

The requirements for the aircraft that became the B-36 were born out of concern about the German advances in Europe. On 11 April 1941 the US Army Air Corps issued a requirement for a very long-range heavy bomber—an aircraft capable of striking targets in Europe from bases in North America. Characteristics desired of the new aircraft were:

450 MPH top speed at 25,000 feet

275 MPH cruising speed

Maximum range of 12,000 miles at 25,000 feet

Service ceiling of 45,000 feet

Bomb capacity was to be 10,000 pounds with a 5,000-mile radius, or for shorter missions, a maximum load of 72,000 pounds.

Requests for proposals for such aircraft were sent to Boeing and Consolidated, with both companies responding by 3 May. However, the response was not encouraging as engineers at neither company were able to meet all the requirements set forth. Thus, on 19 August 1941, the Chief of the Army Air Forces, Major General George Brett, met with the Air Staff and Assistant Secretary of War Robert Lovett and revised the requirements, settling on specifications more technically feasible.

The new requirements set the cruising speed at 240 to 300 mph, service ceiling at 40,000 feet, range at 10,000 miles, and combat radius of 4,000 miles with a 10,000-pound bomb load. These revised specifications were provided to Boeing, Consolidated and Douglas.

At this stage, Boeing had experience with very large aircraft with its XB-15, Consolidated with the XPB2Y Coronado, and Douglas with the XB-19—the largest bomber built for the United States until the XB-36.

All three firms submitted proposals in September 1941, with the Air Forces selecting the Consolidated offering. Contract W535-AC-22532 was issued on 15 November calling for the construction of two XB-36 prototypes, with delivery for the first to occur in May 1944, with the second following in November 1944.

Detailed design work and construction of a mockup began at Convair's San Diego facility, where it was planned to produce the prototypes. Trouble soon arose, however, when it was learned that the Pratt and Whitney R-4360 engines that were to power the aircraft would be significantly heavier than had been previously estimated. This in turn meant that less weight was available for fuel, which thus meant that the range would fall short of the desired 10,000 miles. In an effort to remedy this, it was decided to utilize a new 208-volt, 400-cycle, 3-phase electrical system rather than the DC electrical system that was norm in aircraft of the age. The AC system offered a significant weight advantage over a DC system, but even with this and

eliminating equipment deemed of marginal utility, the mockup showed that the design would fall short of the range goal. However despite this, the mockup, which had been inspected in July, was approved in September.

In the interim, however, it was decided to shift work on the massive bomber to Consolidated's Fort Worth facility. The mockup and 200 members of Consolidated's engineering staff moved east. This move was but one of the many circumstances that would delay completion of the XB-36. The government placed higher priority at the Fort Worth plant on production of the B-24 Liberator, and its cargo-carrying sibling, the C-87, as well as the B-32 heavy bomber. In hopes of speeding the B-36 project, Consolidated proposed the development of the XC-99 cargo aircraft.

The massive cargo plane would use the same wing, landing gear and powerplant structure as the bomber, without the complications inherent in weapons systems. The hope was that work on the cargo plane could move quickly, thus becoming an unofficial test bed for those components. The government liked the idea of the cargo plane, but ironically stipulated that work on it should proceed after the first XB-36 was completed, thereby defeating Consolidated's intent.

In March 1943 Consolidated Aircraft merged with Vultee Aircraft, becoming Consolidated Vultee Aircraft Corporation. Though used informally almost immediately, the name did not formally change to Convair until 29 April 1954.

Well before the first XB-36 took flight, on 23 July 1943 a letter of intent for 100 production bombers was issued. This haste was in response to Japanese gains in the Pacific, and a hope to bomb mainland Japan from Hawaii or even Alaska. By August of the next year, the Allied progress in the Pacific, as well as the resolution of many of the problems in the B-29 program, negated the previously pressing need. Nonetheless, the army issued the production contract for the 100 aircraft on the letter of intent. This contract was valued at $160 million, and it stipulated that the entire group of production aircraft was to be delivered between August 1945 and October 1946.

Rollout of the XB-36 at last occurred on 8 September 1945, but it did not take to the air until almost a year later, when on 8 August 1946 it lifted off with Beryl Erickson at the controls.

Test flights revealed that the bomber's top speed was only 320 MPH, and it was plagued by both engine cooling and propeller vibration problems.

The second XB-36 was completed as a YB-36 per an Army order of 7 April 1945. The YB-36 differed from the XB-36 in several details, most apparent being the utilization of a raised greenhouse flight deck and nose-mounted gun installation, in lieu of the XB-36 's conventional cockpit arrangement.

The YB-36 first flew on 4 December 1947. In May of the following year the main landing gear, which to this point utilized single 110-inch tires beneath each wing, was replaced with four-wheel, dual-tandem landing gear of the type used on production aircraft. Wheel loadings were so high with the original gear that only three airfields could accommodate the massive bomber with full load. With the improved landing gear, the loads imposed on runways were not greater than those of the B-29. In October 1956 the YB-36 reentered the Fort Worth plant to be converted into an RB-36E, and would operate in that configuration until 1957, at which time it was transferred to the Air Force Museum. Subsequently, and after the acquisition of a second example, the former YB-36 was de-accessioned and sold for scrap.

The first of the production aircraft, B-36A 44-92004, actually took to the air almost four months before the YB-36. Roll-out for the B-36A was in June 1947, with the first flight on 28 August 1947. That first flight was around the pattern at Fort Worth. Its second and final flight was to Wright Field, where it was subjected to structural tests, intentionally destroying the aircraft. The first operational B-36A, 44-92005, was delivered in 1948. The twenty-second and final B-36A was delivered in February 1949. Lacking defensive armament, the B-36A aircraft were used primarily as operational training and testing aircraft, chiefly at Carswell Air Force Base, conveniently next door to the B-36 factory in Fort Worth.

In the U.S. strategic bomber arsenal, the Convair B-36 Peacemaker succeeded the famous heavy bomber of World War II, the Boeing B-29 Superfortress. As impressive in size as the B-29 was, the B-36 dwarfed it, as seen in this photo of a B-29 and the XB-36-CF. (National Museum of the United States Air Force)

The next model, the B-36B, featured improved, more powerful, and regrettably heavier R-4360-41 engines rather than the R-4360-25 engines of the earlier models. This boosted horsepower from 3,000 to 3,500 per engine. The B-36B was also outfitted with a full defensive armament suite of 16 20mm cannon mounted in pairs housed in six retractable turrets plus a nose and tail installation. Structural improvements meant that maximum bomb load of the B-36B climbed to 86,000-pounds, allowing it to carry two of the T-12 Cloudmaker demolition bombs.

Original plans had called for 73 B-36B aircraft to be produced, but eleven of those were completed instead as B-36D. Of the B-36B aircraft that were built, bomb bay number one in each of the final 47 assembled were factory-equipped to carry a Mark III Fat Man atomic bomb.

Even with the more powerful engines, the B-36B was slower than desired, with an average cruising speed of 300 mph, and a top speed of 381 mph. In an effort to improve on this, Convair set to work on a proposed B-36C, which was to be powered by Variable Discharge Turbine (VDT) engines.

The B-36C program proved unworkable, and an alternative solution was found in the form of adding two pairs of General Electric J47-GE-19 engines, one pair beneath each wing. The J47s were modified so that they would burn conventional aviation gas rather than jet fuel, eliminating the need for dual, and perhaps confusing, fuel supply systems. The initial configuration of bomber powered by six piston engines and four jet engines was designated the B-36D. Doors on the front of the jet engine air intakes could be closed to shut off airflow and lessen drag when the jets were not being used, as during long cruise flights.

Another notable change brought with the D model was magnesium-covered control surfaces, rather than fabric-covered control surfaces. Additionally, a new style of folding, so called "snap action" bomb bay doors were introduced, replacing the rolling doors reminiscent of those found on the B-24, used previously. Ultimately, the Air Force rostered 76-newly built B-36D aircraft, which were augmented by the conversion of all existing B-36Bs to B-36D configuration. The first four such conversions were done at Fort Worth, with the balance of the conversions being performed in San Diego.

A photoreconnaissance variant of the B-36D was also operational, fittingly designated the RB-36D. The position of bomb bay number one of the reconnaissance variant was filled with a 16-foot long pressurized compartment housing up to 14 cameras, as well as a darkroom permitting the film cartridges to be reloaded in flight. This pressurized area is what required the most significant change to the aircraft. What normally would have been bomb bay bulkheads instead had to be pressure domes, and the typical magnesium covering of the area was not strong enough to withstand the pressurization, so aluminum was used instead. The shiny aluminum contrasted with the dull magnesium of the surrounding area. Twenty-four RB-36Ds were built; all new from the ground up, although seven had originally been ordered as B-36B, but were not completed in bomber configuration. As originally produced, the RB-36D could not carry an offensive bomb load, although bomb bay number two was configured to drop photoflash bombs.

In late 1955, however, the decision was made to modify the reconnaissance aircraft so that they could drop nuclear weapons, while retaining the photographic capabilities. A bomb bay was installed in the same space that a conventional B-36D number four bomb bay was located (that space previously being filled with Electronic Countermeasures equipment). Bomb bays two and three, previously covered by a single set of doors (bomb bay 3 containing a 3,000 gallon auxiliary fuel tank), had their doors changed. A single door system covered bay three and the new bay four, while a 16-foot set of doors was provided for bay two.

RB-36D 44-92090 recorded the longest known flight of a B-36 or variant. Lifting off at 9:05 AM 14 January 1951, its landing gear tires did not again touch a runway until 12:35 PM 16 January; 51-1/2 hours later.

To add even more reconnaissance aircraft to the Strategic Air Command (SAC) inventory, the B-36A aircraft, along with the YB-36, were converted to RB-36E. This was an extensive and intrusive process, requiring many new parts. The twenty-two RB-36E aircraft were constructed in this way, all but one moving down the assembly line with the new-build B-36D models. During the conversion, for J47 engines were added and the original R-4360-25 engines were replaced with R-4260-41 models. Defensive armament was added as well, the B-36A aircraft previously lacking this.

The B-36F was an improved model, featuring R-4360-53 engines with a maximum output of 3,800 horsepower each. Ordered 13 April 1949, the B-36F first flew 18 November 1950. Fifteen of the type, along with 19 RB-36Fs, had been on that initial order, with a follow-on order in 1950 calling for a further 19 bombers and five RB-36F aircraft. All 24 RB-36Fs were delivered to the 7th Bomb Wing at Carswell, and three of them were lost there, two in ground accidents and one that landed short, killing seven crewmembers.

The 24 RB-36Fs were substantially equivalent to the RB-36D, albeit with the mechanical improvements commensurate with the B-36F model.

Boeing's B-52 Stratofortress, the mockup for which was completed in 1947, clearly marked the way of the future for heavy bombers. Convair, wanting to keep their business, offered unsolicited to the Air Force an alternative design, the B-36G. This aircraft, like the B-52, had swept wings and was powered by jet engines. The Air Force was sufficiently intrigued to, on 15 March 1951, approve the conversion of two incomplete B-36F aircraft (49-2676 and 49-2684) to B-36G configuration. At about the same time the designation of B-36G was superseded by YB-60, owing to the radical changes to the airframe.

The first YB-60 flew for the first time on 18 April 1952, three days after the first flight of the YB-52. Although the YB-60 was cheaper, due to the commonalty with parts already in production, the Boeing offered superior performance. The YB-60 flight test program was halted after only 66 hours, and the second YB-60 was cancelled when it was 95% complete. The Air Force formally accepted both aircraft on 1 July 1954, and scrapping began the same day.

With 83 built, the B-36H was a significant step forward in terms of quantity production of the bomber. Mechanically, the B-36H was little changed from the B-36F, with the most substantial changes being a revised flight deck accommodating a second flight engineer, and relocation of the bombing/navigation electronic gear into the pressurized forward compartment. This relocation permitted in-flight maintenance.

Other changes incident with the introduction of the B-36H included square-tipped propellers, lessening vibration, and an improved AN/APG-41 gun laying tail radar, which began to be installed at serial number 51-5472. Chaff dispensers, either the A-6 or A-7 models, also were fitted. The B-36H first flew on 5 April 1952, although deliveries did not begin until December, owing to the Air Force electing not to accept new aircraft pending correction of flaws in pressure bulkheads of some B-36F models.

In addition to the 83 straight bombers, 73 RB-36H reconnaissance aircraft were produced. These aircraft, although outfitted like the RB-36F, were mechanically identical to the B-36H.

The final production variant of the B-36 program was the B-36J, which also notably were the last propeller-driven heavy bombers acquired by SAC. The B-36J had two additional wing fuel tanks, adding 2,770 gallons of fuel, and strengthened landing gear, permitting a gross take off weight of 410,000 pounds. Externally, a single long radome replaced the twin radomes used on the APG-41A gun laying radar introduced on the B-36H. Thirty-three B-36J models were produced, the first flying in July 1953, and rollout of the final B-36J, 52-2827 occurring 10 August 1954.

The final 14 were completed as Featherweight III aircraft. The Featherweight program, introduced in January 1954, was aimed reducing the weight of the aircraft in order to gain more range and altitude, specifically with the goal of delivering hydrogen bombs. The B-36 notably was not equipped for in-flight refueling, making such efforts of considerable importance. Three variations of the Featherweight program were developed. Featherweight I aircraft were shorn of their conventional bomb racks and retractable turrets. Featherweight II aircraft retained their guns and conventional bomb racks, but as many drag-producing protuberances as possible were removed, and flush replacements for the sighting blisters were procured. The gun turrets were modified to permit relatively rapid removal. These changes resulted in a weight reduction of 4,800 pounds, even with the turrets retained, and remarkably resulted in a 25% increase in range.

The most extensive modification was the previously mentioned Featherweight III. In this configuration, all defensive armament but for the tail guns was eliminated, and most of the sighting blisters removed, as was the astrodome atop the cockpit. The bulk of the crew comfort items, such as bunks, galley, insulation and sound deadening material, were deleted as well. Without guns, the number of crew could be reduced, but with the removal of the insulation, provision had to be added for the use of heated flying suits by the remaining crewmembers. All told, 15,000 pounds of weight were dropped. The operational B-36 aircraft were all subjected to some form of the Featherweight program, with the Featherweight III aircraft enjoying a range increase of 25 to 40%, depending on base model of aircraft modified. In addition to increased range, top speeds were raised, as were ceiling, officially reaching 47,000 feet, although some crews reported operating well over 50,000 feet.

XB-36

YB-36

XC-99 (final)

B-36A

B-36B

B-36C

B-36D

RB-36D

GRB-36F and RF-84K

B-36J III

YB-60

Engine Data

Make:	Pratt and Whitney
Model:	R-4360-41
Type:	28-cylinder, four row, air-cooled radial
Displacement:	4,360 cubic inches
Bore:	5.75 inches
Stroke:	6 inches
Diameter:	55 inches
Length:	96.5 inches
Compression ratio:	6.7:1
Gasoline grade:	115/145 octane
Fuel consumption, max:	195 gallons per horsepower/hour
Supercharger:	Gear-driven single stage, 6.374:1 ratio
Turbosupercharger:	2x General Electric B-1 per engine
Weight:	3,404 lbs.
Maximum rpm:	2,700
Maximum horsepower:	3,500
Maximum torque:	7,506 pound-feet.

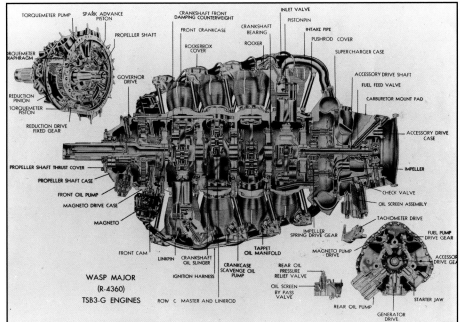

Top left: The XB-36 and subsequent production B-36s were powered by six Pratt & Whitney R-4360 Wasp Major radial engines in a pusher configuration. Development of this engine, considered the most sophisticated mass-produced U.S. radial engine, began in 1940. **Above right:** A Pratt & Whitney cutaway schematic of the R-4360 Wasp Major illustrates the one-piece forged steel crankshaft running though the crankcase. To the rear of the engine is the propeller shaft and reduction gear case, while at the front is the accessory drive case. (National Museum of the United States Air Force, all) **Above left:** The R-4360 engine had 28 cylinders, arranged in spiral fashion around the crankcase with four rows, seven cylinders per row. This staggered arrangement facilitated cooling and resulted in a relatively narrow profile for the engine, as viewed here from the side.

The XB-36

The XB-36 prototype, serial number 42-13570, climbs above Lake Worth and the Convair factory and Carswell Air Force Base complex at Fort Worth, Texas. The aircraft made its maiden flight on 8 August 1946, 11 months later than originally anticipated. To the lower right is the runway complex that served the factory and the air base, and to the top of the right side of the runways are some of the buildings of Carswell. (Stan Piet collection)

As indicated in this photograph of a model dated 14 November 1941, the original design for the Consolidated Aircraft Model 36 called for twin vertical tails and rudders. It also featured six rear-facing engines with pusher propellers and a wingspan of 230 feet. (San Diego Air and Space Museum)

K36-003
CONSOLIDATED AIRCRAFT CORP
MODEL 36
DISPLAY MODEL.
11-14-41

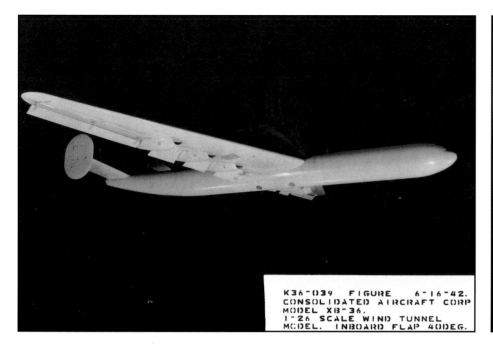

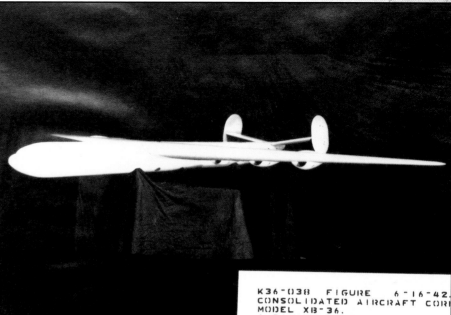

Top left: A 1/26-scale wind-tunnel test model of the Model XB-36 was photographed in 16 June 1942. Unlike the engine nacelles on the actual XB-36 and production B-36s, the front ends of the six engine nacelles did not extend to the leading edges of the wings. **Top right:** In a front left view of the wind-tunnel model of the XB-36, the horizontal stabilizers, which supported the twin tail structures, exhibit a pronounced dihedral. The top of the cockpit canopy at this stage of design was flush with the top deck of the fuselage. **Above:** Prior to Consolidated Aircraft's merger with Vultee to form Convair, Consolidated fabricated a full-scale wooden mockup of the XB-36 at its San Diego, California, plant. The mockup is seen in a July 1942 photo. Only the port wing was present on the mockup. (San Diego Air and Space Museum, all)

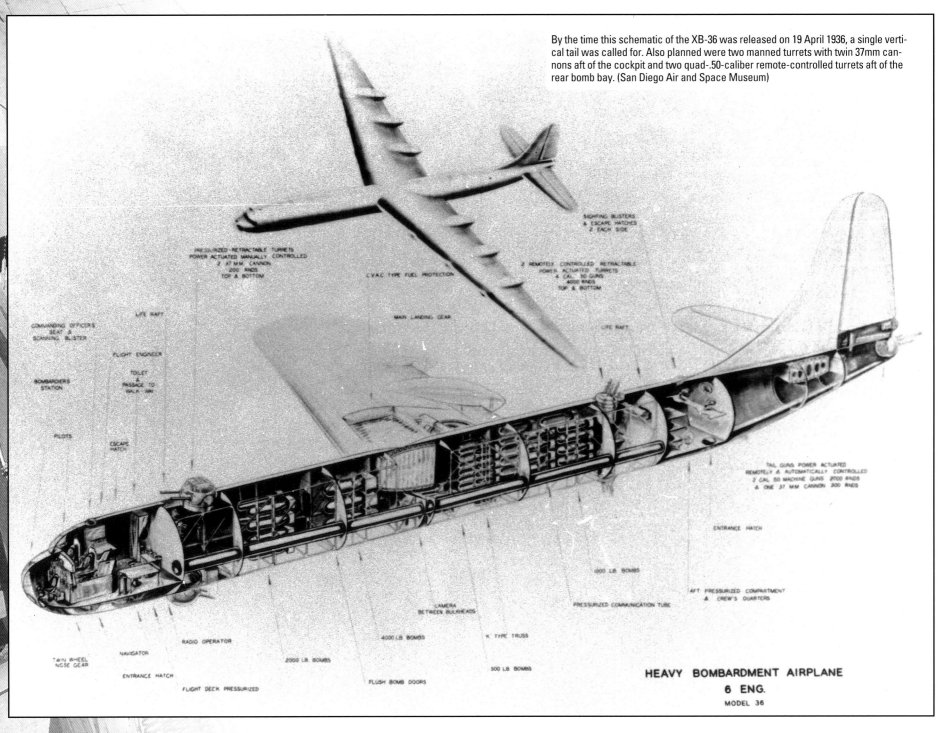

By the time this schematic of the XB-36 was released on 19 April 1936, a single vertical tail was called for. Also planned were two manned turrets with twin 37mm cannons aft of the cockpit and two quad-.50-caliber remote-controlled turrets aft of the rear bomb bay. (San Diego Air and Space Museum)

HEAVY BOMBARDMENT AIRPLANE
6 ENG.
MODEL 36

A technician stands below one of the XB-36 wind-tunnel models. In this incarnation of the design, the fronts of the engine nacelles, equipped with large air intakes, were well aft of the leading edge of the wing. However, this version had a single vertical tail. (American Aviation Historical Society)

The status of work on the XB-36 was documented in a 1 May 1946 photograph taken inside the Experimental Building at Convair's Fort Worth plant. Large sections of the leading edges of the wings had not yet been installed. Extensive scaffolding was used. (San Diego Air and Space Museum)

When this photo of the XB-36 was taken in August 1945, the plane had been rolled temporarily out of the Experimental Building. Noticeable are the huge main landing gear and the absence of the control surfaces and large sections of the wings. (San Diego Air and Space Museum)

Work on the XB-36 proceeds in the Experimental Building at Convair's Fort Worth plant in the summer of 1945. The clear panels of the cockpit canopy had protective coverings except for the removable side panels. Aft of the canopy is the opening for the astrodome. (San Diego Air and Space Museum)

By the time this photo of the XB-36 was taken, main landing gear doors had been installed. Besides being bulky, the main-gear tires concentrated the massive weight of the plane on a small area, and thus the plane could land only on highly reinforced runways. (Stan Piet collection)

Top left: The XB-36 undergoes an early test flight with its landing gear lowered. As originally configured, the plane had a single 110-inch tire on each main-gear strut. The main-gear doors were not fitted during the initial flights, but the nose-gear doors were present. (National Museum of the United States Air Force) **Top right:** A man standing next to the port main landing gear between engine number three and the fuselage gives a sense of scale of the huge, 110-inch tires, the largest that Goodyear ever produced. Each main-gear wheel was equipped with dual multiple-disk brakes. (National Museum of the United States Air Force) **Above left:** During a flight on 26 March 1947, the XB-36's starboard main landing gear actuator failed while the main gear was being retracted. The pilot, Beryl Erickson, brought the plane in for a successful emergency landing. The starboard gear is viewed from aft. (San Diego Air and Space Museum) **Above right:** The starboard main gear on the XB-36 is seen from the front after the emergency landing. The flight could have ended tragically because the main gear broke several hydraulic and fuel lines when the gear actuator failed and the main strut swung down violently. (San Diego Air and Space Museum)

Top: Eventually, the XB-36's oversized, single-wheel landing gear was replaced by eight-wheel main gears. This arrangement allowed for a broader distribution of the aircraft's weight on a runway; as a result, the plane could operate from more air bases. (American Aviation Historical Society, both) **Above:** A buzz number, BM-570, was now present on the fuselage of the XB-36. Buzz numbers were a postwar means of identifying U.S. aircraft, particularly those guilty of buzzing cities. "BM" stood for B-36, and "570" was the last three digits of the serial number.

Above left: The eight-wheel main gear on the starboard side of the XB-36 is viewed from the front. The wheels were much smaller than the originally mounted 110-inch single wheels. The main landing gear struts were of a different design than the original, single-wheel struts. Later, a similar main landing gear would be developed for production B-36s but with four 56-inch tires rather than eight tires. (American Aviation Historical Society) **Top right:** Convair experimented with a tracked landing gear on the XB-36 to test its applicability to ultra-heavy aircraft. As seen on the starboard main gear, steel-reinforced rubber tracks revolving around rollers were mounted on a frame on each side of the strut. (National Museum of the United States Air Force) **Above right:** The tracked nose landing gear is viewed from the starboard side with the XB-36 raised on jacks; a tow bar is fastened to the front of the nose gear. Tests with this gear were successful, but the tracked landing gear was never implemented on the production B-36s. (National Museum of the United States Air Force)

Top: With the experimental tracked landing gear installed on all three struts, the XB-36 is poised on a runway, engines running. Ground crewmen are checking the left main landing gear. The XB-36 performed a number of taxiing and takeoff/landing tests with the tracked landing gear at Carswell Air Force Base in early 1950. **Above:** When the XB-36 was introduced, there were only three runways in the world with sufficient length and strength to support the weight of this ultra-heavy bomber. The tracked landing gear was proposed as a means of spreading out the ground pressure of the landing gear, in order to allow the bomber to use existing, unimproved runways. (National Museum of the United States Air Force, both)

Top: The tracked gear on the XB-36 exerted 57 psi of ground pressure, compared to 156 psi for the production B-36's landing gear. The tracked gear would have facilitated operations from a wider variety of airfields, including those that were hastily prepared.
Above: The XB-36 runs up its engines during tests of the tracked landing gear at Barksdale Air Force Base, Louisiana, in January 1950. The first flight with the tracked gear was two months later. The tracks made a horrible screeching sound when they were turning. (National Museum of the United States Air Force, both)

The aircraft assigned U.S. Army Air Forces serial number 42-13571 originally was to have been the second XB-36 but was redesignated YB-36-CF in April 1945. The prefix Y stood for preproduction, since it was intended that the YB-36-CF be built closer to production standards than the XB-36. Conspicuous differences in the YB-36 compared to the XB-36 included a new, raised flight deck and canopy, a revised forward crew compartment, redesigned rear bomb bays, and allowances for a nose turret. The YB-36 is shown here with its BM-571 buzz number and its original 110-inch main landing gear tires. (Stan Piet collection)

Top left: Eventually, the single, large, main landing gear tires and wheels were exchanged for multiple-wheel gears similar to those used on the XB-36, but with four wheels instead of eight per landing gear, as seen on the XB-36 on display at the Air Force Museum. **Top right:** The well-weathered YB-36 on display at the Air Force Museum rested next to a Junkers Ju 88. The General Electric J47 jet pods under the wings evidently were added when the YB-36 was remanufactured into an RB-36E long-range reconnaissance bomber in 1950. **Above left:** The canopy of the YB-36, displayed at the Air Force Museum, were painted aluminum. The clear dome aft of the cockpit was removed and the opening was plugged. Next to the YB-36 is a McDonnell XF-85 Goblin, developed as a parasite fighter for the B-36. **Above right:** The tail of the YB-36 is viewed from the port side during its residence at the Air Force Museum. The Air Force frequently used this aircraft as the first one to undergo a number of modification programs, and it had 1,952.5 flight hours when it was retired in 1957. (American Aviation Historical Society, all)

The XC-99

The XC-99-1-CO cargo plane (Convair Model 37) was a development of the B-36 program that employed the bomber's wings, engines, empennage, and landing gear along with a wide-body fuselage. With a cargo space of 16,000 cubic feet on two decks, the plane was designed to transport some 100,000 pounds of cargo or 400 combat-equipped troops. Up to 300 patients on litters also could be transported. Only one XC-99, serial number 43-52436, was produced. (Stan Piet collection)

Unlike the B-36, which had large sections of magnesium skin in addition to sections of aluminum-alloy skin, the XC-99's skin was almost all aluminum. In this photo of the plane under construction, the skin of the fuselage has a very wrinkly appearance. (National Museum of the United States Air Force)

The XC-99 undergoes construction work on 11 March 1947, eight months before its maiden flight. The plane was assembled at Convair's San Diego plant, although the wings and certain other assemblies were fabricated at the Fort Worth factory. (National Museum of the United States Air Force)

F37-323   3-11-47
CONSOLIDATED VULTEE
XC-99 - RIGHT SIDE VIEW

Top: A B-36 closely tails the XC-99, demonstrating the similarities and disparities in the two related aircraft. The XC-99 had an overall length of 182.5 feet, while the B-36 was a bit over 162 feet long. The fuselage of the XC-99 was much taller than that of the B-36.
Above left: The logo on the forward fuselage of the XC-99 reads "Convair" between the wings of an eagle, below which is "XC-99." The plane was ahead of its time, as wide-body cargo aircraft would not come of age until two decades later with the Boeing 747.
Above right: The XC-99 comes in for a landing at Lindberg Field, San Diego. Visible below the aft part of the fuselage is an extended tail bumper. As built, the XC-99 had single 110-inch tires for the main landing gear. Later, four-tire gear assemblies would replace these. (National Museum of the United States Air Force, all)

By the time this photo of the XC-99 was taken, four-wheel main landing gear assemblies had replaced the original single 110-inch-tire versions. Gone was the Convair XC-99 logo, and "United States Air Force" was marked on the side of the fuselage. (National Museum of the United States Air Force)

Above left: The worker hanging from the side of the vertical tail of the XC-99 and the men steadying the line he is attached to provide a sense of the massive scale of the aircraft. The tail cone of the fuselage was one of the few magnesium components on the exterior of the XC-99. To the right is a special portable work stand developed for the use of workmen operating on the vertical tail of the XC-99. Similar stands were used with the Convair B-36. (Stan Piet collection) **Above right:** Workmen make adjustments in one of the cargo levels of the XC-99. There were two cargo levels in the aircraft, stacked one atop the other. Loading of cargo was accomplished through two powered sliding doors on the bottom of the fuselage. Supplementing the aft sliding door and located aft of it were other access doors and two sets of clamshell doors. Four electric hoists facilitated moving cargo between the decks. (San Diego Air and Space Museum)

Top left: The XC-99 had flat-tipped propellers, which had the advantage of causing less buffeting to the flattened sides of the fuselage. This photo was taken before the nose radome was installed on the plane in June 1953, a feature that appears in the subsequent photos of the plane. (American Aviation Historical Society) **Top right:** By 1954, when assigned to the 1700th Air Transport Group, Kelly Field, Texas, the XC-99 had a white area above the cockpit to deflect sun rays to cool the cockpit. The arrow insignia on the tail marked "SAAMA" was that of the San Antonio Air Material Area. **Above left:** The radome on the nose contained a weather radar set with a maximum range exceeding 200 miles and a weight of 250 pounds. While based at Kelly Field, the XC-99 made bi-weekly supply flights to and from McClellan Air Force Base, California, in support of the B-36 bomber force. **Above right:** From its retirement in 1957 until 2004 the XC-99 resided at Kelly Field, at times on display in a weed-choked field, all the time slowly deteriorating. In 2004 the aircraft was moved to Wright-Patterson Air Force Base, where the major components are stored outside the restoration facility. (National Museum of the United States Air Force, three)

The B-36A was the first production model of the bomber. Twenty-two examples were produced. It was in most respects quite similar to the YB-36, and, in fact, the first B-36A, serial number 44-92004, was later redesignated the YB-36A. The B-36As were not combat-ready, as none were equipped with the full defensive weapons suite. Rather, this model of B-36 was mainly used to train crews, identify and resolve the mechanical glitches in the bombers, and test its operational performance and bomb-delivery potential. Shown here is the third production B-36A, B-36A-1-CF serial number 44-92006. (Stan Piet collection)

The first B-36A, 44-92004, first took to the air on 28 August 1947, almost four months before the YB-36's first flight. The B-36A made only two flights. It reportedly was re-designated the YB-36A and flown to Wright Field, Ohio, for use as a static-test plane. (American Aviation Historical Society)

Above left: The first B-36A is undergoing static structural tests at Wright Field. Loads were applied to the surfaces of the bomber to gauge their strength under stress in order to determine its capabilities. The plane ultimately was destroyed during the tests, as intended. (Stan Piet collection) **Top right:** The fourth B-36A, serial number 44-92007, rests on a tarmac near a hangar. The B-36A had four bomb bays with electrically operated sliding doors that moved by means of rollers on curved, recessed tracks on the sides of the fuselage. The forward and rear bomb bays had single doors with tracks on the left side of the fuselage. The second and third bomb bays each had two doors with tracks on each side of the fuselage, an arrangement necessary because of the positions of the wings. **Above right:** A close look at this photo of the first B-36A discloses that the door of the forward bomb bay was open. The magnesium fuselage skin on the sides of the bomb bays had a matte appearance, while the aluminum skin on the forward end of the fuselage was shiny. (American Aviation Historical Society)

Top: On Convair B-36A-1-CF 44-92006, all four bomb-bay doors are open, and the starboard doors of bomb bays two and three are visible on the side of the fuselage. The open doors for the other two bomb bays are not in view, being raised on the port side of the fuselage. **Above:** A B-36A presents its front to the photographer on a runway, highlighting the shape of the bombardier's clear nose. The two air inlets at the front of each engine nacelle admitted cooling air for the engines as well as air for the intercoolers, the oil coolers, and the turbosuperchargers. (National Museum of the United States Air Force, both)

The Air Force enjoyed arranging publicity photos comparing the gigantic B-36 with smaller aircraft, such as B-36A-1-CF 44-92006 with a Lockheed P-80 Shooting Star resting alongside it. Below the B-36A's cockpit, a round access hatch has been opened. (American Aviation Historical Society)

Top Left: B-36A-1-CF 44-92006 is viewed from below. The bomb-bay doors are partially open. The contrast in sheen between the magnesium skin panels along the bomb bays and the aluminum-alloy skin panels on the front and rear portions of the fuselage is evident. (American Aviation Historical Society) **Top Right:** In a side view of 44-92006 taken within a moment of the preceding photo, the doors of bomb bays one and four are open, but the doors of the other two bays are only partially open. The bulge to the front of bomb bay one is the radome for the AN/APQ-23 radar. (American Aviation Historical Society) **Above:** The flight crew and support personnel pose in front of a B-36A along with ancillary equipment, including fuel trucks, a Cletrac hitched to a trailer containing what appear to be oxygen tanks, an ambulance, and a bomb truck hitched to two fully laden bomb trailers. (National Museum of the United States Air Force)

Personnel are assembled in front of B-36A serial number 44-92015 as another B-36 flies overhead. Although no guns were mounted in the tail turret, a dome representing the ball of the turret is present on the tail, above which is the radome for the fire-control radar. (National Museum of the United States Air Force)

The second production B-36 produced, B-36A-1-CF USAF serial number 44-92005, flies low over an airfield, landing gear lowered. The tailskid is extended; this would protect the bottom rear of the fuselage should the aircraft experience an extreme nose-up landing or takeoff. (American Aviation Historical Society)

Top left: A crewmember looks out of the open access port of B-36A-10-CF 44-92015. A close-up view is offered of the unit emblem of the 7th Bombardment Wing. The motto "mors ab alto" is Latin for "death from above." The bombardier's flat window has a wiper.

Top right: Although the first B-36A had been dubbed *The City of Fort Worth* in honor of the place where these planes were produced, once that plane had been relegated to static testing, B-36A-10-CF 44-92015 was given that name, which is painted on the fuselage. **Above left:** In the background, B-36A-10-CF serial number 44-92012 is undergoing maintenance or modification work. The rudder has been removed, and work stands are pushed up next to the fuselage. In the foreground are the wing and several nacelles of another B-36. **Above right:** The black triangle on the vertical tail of B-36A-15-CF serial number 44-92025 was the postwar tactical symbol for the Eighth Air Force, and the circular marking to the front of the lower forward corner of the triangle is the insignia of the Eighth Air Force. (American Aviation Historical Society, all)

The BM-022 buzz number on this B-36A-15-CF identifies it as serial number 44-92022, accepted by the Air Force in September 1948. The B-36As were delivered in bare-metal finish; the fabric-covered control surfaces were painted with a matte aluminum dope. (American Aviation Historical Society)

B-36A-15-CF flies low over Lowry Air Force Base at Denver, Colorado. The spike-shaped feature at the center of the vertical fin is sometimes seen in photos of B-36s and appears to have been skin panels that were of a different sheen than surrounding ones. (American Aviation Historical Society)

Left: B-36A-10-CF serial number 44-92014 runs up its 3,000-horsepower Pratt & Whitney R-4360-25 Wasp Major engines prior to takeoff. The buzz number BM-014 includes the last three digits of the serial number, and the last two digits of that number, 14, are faintly painted on the main landing gear door. Marked prominently on the nose landing gear door is "NO SMOKING WITHIN 100 FT." **Right:** The tail of B-36A-10-CF 44-92014 is viewed from the starboard side as the plane warms its engines. The tail bumper is lowered below the fuselage. Although the B-36As lacked defensive armaments, the clear domes for the gunners were installed; two of them are visible here. Gunners included in the crews of B-36As served chiefly as spotters to check the operation of the engines, landing gear, and such. (American Aviation Historical Society, both)

A dummy tail turret and radome were installed on the B-36A, as seen on B-36A-10-CF 44-92014. Once the B-36s were fitted out with defensive armaments, the tail turret would receive two 20mm cannons, and an APG-3 radar for sighting the tail turret would be installed, including an antenna in the radome. Above the radome, the lower part of the starboard side of the fabric-covered rudder is in view. (American Aviation Historical Society)

B-36 serial numbers

Serial	Model	Serial	Model
42-13570	XB-36-CF	50-1091 through 50-1097	B-36H-5-CF
42-13571	YB-36-CF [1]	50-1098 through 50-1099	RB-36F-10-CF
43-52436	XC-99-1-CO	50-1100 through 50-1102	RB-36F-15-CF
44-92004 through 44-92006	B-36A-1-CF	50-1103 through 50-1105	RB-36H-1-CF
44-92007 through 44-92011	B-36A-5-CF	50-1106 through 50-1110	RB-36H-5-CF
44-92012 through 44-92017	B-36A-10-CF	51-13717 through 51-13719	RB-36H-20-CF
44-92018 through 44-92025	B-36A-15-CF	51-13720 through 51-13725	RB-36H-25-CF
44-92026 through 44-92037	B-36B-1-CF	51-13726 through 51-13731	RB-36H-30-CF
44-92038 through 44-92049	B-36B-5-CF	51-13732 through 51-13737	RB-36H-35-CF
44-92050 through 44-92064	B-36B-10-CF	51-13738 through 51-13741	RB-36H-40-CF
44-92065 through 44-92079	B-36B-15-CF	51-5699 through 51-5705	B-36H-10-CF
44-92080 through 44-92087	B-36B-20-CF	51-5706 through 51-5711	B-36H-15-CF
44-92088 through 44-92094	RB-36D-1-CF	51-5712 through 51-5717	B-36H-20-CF
44-92095 through 44-92098	B-36D-1-CF	51-5718 through 51-5723	B-36H-25-CF
49-2647 through 49-2654	B-36D-5-CF	51-5724 through 51-5729	B-36H-30-CF
49-2655	B-36D-35-CF	51-5730 through 51-5735	B-36H-35-CF
49-2656 through 49-2657	B-36D-15-CF	51-5736 through 51-5742	B-36H-40-CF
49-2655 through 49-2657	B-36D-35-CF	51-5743 through 51-5747	RB-36H-10-CF
49-2658 through 49-2663	B-36D-25-CF	51-5748 through 51-5753	RB-36H-15-CF
49-2664 through 49-2668	B-36D-35-CF	51-5754 through 51-5756	RB-36H-20-CF
49-2669 through 49-2675	B-36F-1-CF	52-1343 through 52-1347	B-36H-45-CF
49-2676	YB-60-1-CF	52-1348 through 52-1353	B-36H-50-CF
49-2677	B-36F-1-CF	52-1354 through 52-1359	B-36H-55-CF
49-2678 through 49-2683	B-36F-5-CF	52-1360 through 52-1366	B-36H-60-CF
49-2684	YB-60-2-CF	52-1367 through 52-1373	RB-36H-45-CF
49-2685	B-36F-5-CF	52-1374 through 52-1380	RB-36H-50-CF
49-2686	RB-36D-5-CF	52-1381 through 52-1386	RB-36H-55-CF
49-2687 through 49-2693	RB-36D-10-CF	52-1387 through 52-1392	RB-36H-60-CF
49-2694 through 49-2697	RB-36D-15-CF	52-2210 through 52-2221	B-36J-1-CF
49-2698 through 49-2702	RB-36D-20-CF	52-2222 through 52-2226	B-36J-5-CF
49-2703 through 49-2711	RB-36F-1-CF	52-2812 through 52-2813	B-36J-5-CF
49-2712 through 49-2721	RB-36F-5-CF	52-2814 through 52-2818	B-36J-5-CF [2]
50-1064 through 50-1073	B-36F-10-CF	52-2819 through 52-2827	B-36J-10-CF [3]
50-1074 through 50-1082	B-36F-15-CF		
50-1083 through 50-1090	B-36H-1-CF		

1. Later converted to RB-36E-5-CF
2. Completed as Featherweight III
3. Completed as Featherweight III

The B-36B

The B-36B was the first fully operational and combat-ready model of the B-36. Improvements over the B-36A included the R-4360-41 Wasp Major engines, increased bomb capacity, improved performance, and a full complement of defensive armaments. Here, B-36B-1-CF serial number 44-92028 of the 7th Bombardment Wing of the Eighth Air Force, photographed at Carswell Air Force Base, Texas, around 1949, displays the wing's emblem on the forward part of the fuselage and bright red paint, for high visibility should the plane crash in arctic terrain, on the vertical tail and outer portions of the wings. This red paint was part of the Global Electronics Modification (GEM) Program, a series of modifications to better suit the B-36 and other aircraft for operating and navigating over polar regions. (Stan Piet collection)

Above left: Convair factory workers install windshield wipers for the canopy windscreen of a B-36B. To the front of the black antiglare panel is the nose turret. Only the left 20mm cannon has been installed in the turret. The body of the turret comprised a large shield that could be turned from side to side, thus achieving traverse of the guns, and, set into the large shield, a smaller shield that pivoted so as to elevate or depress with the guns. **Top right:** Workers at Convair's Fort Worth plant place windshield wipers on another B-36B on which the nose turret has not yet been installed. Protective film on the clear panels of the canopy and bombardier's nose will be removed when the plane is completed. **Above right:** The B-36B had four top turrets, mounted side by side in pairs, each with two 20mm cannons, which retracted into two bays when not in use. The two bays with their doors opened are visible in this photo aft of the cockpit and to the front of the vertical tail. (San Diego Air and Space Museum, all)

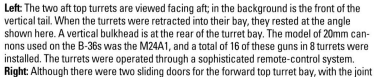

Left: The two aft top turrets are viewed facing aft; in the background is the front of the vertical tail. When the turrets were retracted into their bay, they rested at the angle shown here. A vertical bulkhead is at the rear of the turret bay. The model of 20mm cannons used on the B-36s was the M24A1, and a total of 16 of these guns in 8 turrets were installed. The turrets were operated through a sophisticated remote-control system.
Right: Although there were two sliding doors for the forward top turret bay, with the joint between them being at the top centerline of the fuselage, the aft top turret bay had a single door, which slid on tracks on the starboard side of the fuselage when it was opened. The door is shown open here. The two upper aft gunners' sighting domes are not present, and their openings are temporarily plugged. (American Aviation Historical Society, both)

Above left: Twin M24A1 cannons have been mounted in the tail turret of this B-36B. Slots in the hemispherical gun shield allowed for the elevation of the two cannons. A gunner in the rear pressurized compartment of the fuselage controlled the guns using the APG-3 radar. Two boxes each containing 600 rounds of 20mm ammunition supplied ammunition to the cannons by way of long, flexible feed chutes. (American Aviation Historical Society) **Top right:** A B-36B cruises at low altitude. B-36Bs met most expectations and proved to be a formidable aircraft. For example, in January 1949 a B-36B set a new bomb-load record by dropping two inert 43,000-pound bombs from upwards of 35,000 feet. (American Aviation Historical Society **Above right:** B-36B-5-CF 44-92043 has just been rolled out of Building 4 at Convair's Fort Worth plant. The front end of the plane is raised up on a rolling frame: a procedure always followed when rolling out B-36s in order to drop the tail low enough to clear the door. (National Museum of the United States Air Force)

Convair B-36B-5-CF serial number 44-92042, the 18th B-36B to leave the assembly line, skims low across a body of water. Walkways are marked by lines painted on the horizontal stabilizers, the wings, and the engine nacelles. "UNITED STATES AIR FORCE" is marked in 9-inch-high letters on the forward part of the fuselage; this marking replaced the buzz numbers found in that location earlier. (American Aviation Historical Society)

Left: B-36B-5-CF serial number 44-92039 displays the emblem of the 7th Bombardment Wing on the side of the nose, the Eighth Air Force insignia on the vertical tail, and Arctic Red paint on the empennage and the outer parts of the wings. "USAF" is marked under the wing. (National Museum of the United States Air Force) **Right:** This B-36 is distinguishable as a B model by its nose turret and the extended tail bumper: this bumper was discontinued on new-construction B-36s after the B model but apparently remained present on B-36Bs converted to B-36D configurations. Faintly visible below each side of the "UNITED STATES AIR FORCE" marking on the side of the fuselage is a vertical line marking a forward bomb-bay door track. (Stan Piet collection)

B-36B-10-CF serial number 44-92033 and buzz number BM-033, seen here with Arctic Red paint applied to the empennage and the outer parts of the wings, was the eighth B-36B produced by Convair. The white of the radome of the tail turret contrasts with the adjacent red paint. Even from this angle, the large radome for the AN/APQ-23 radar under the forward portion of the fuselage is highly visible. (NARA)

Convair B-36B-10-CF 44-92033 is viewed from a different angle. The small number 30 on the side of the fuselage just aft of the bombardier's nose was the Convair sequence number, assigned consecutively to production aircraft but not the XB-36 and YB-36. (Stan Piet collection)

The same B-36B-10-CF shown in the two preceding photographs is viewed from the aft starboard quarter. The two vertical lines following the curve of the fuselage just forward of the national insignia are the recessed tracks for the door of the aft top gun turret bay. (Stan Piet collection)

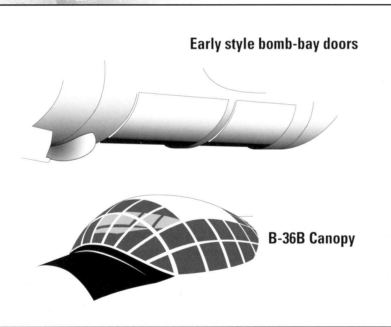

Early style bomb-bay doors

B-36B Canopy

Top: Landing gear retracted, a B-36B comes in low over a populated area. The sight of a B-36 in flight or on the ground was a memorable experience and one that inspired confidence in the United States' ability to defend itself and project its airpower world-wide. (Stan Piet collection) **Above left:** Two features that differentiated the B-36B from later models are illustrated here: the sliding bomb-bay doors on each bomb bay and the smooth contours of the B-model canopy. **Above right:** Ground crewmen are gathered around a civilian to the front of B-36B-1-CF serial number 44-92032. A protective cover is lashed over the cockpit canopy, and the commonly seen warning not to smoke with 100 feet of the plane is on the nose landing gear door. (National Museum of the United States Air Force, two)

Top left: Three B-36s, including one with the triangular Eighth Air Force symbol and two with Arctic Red paint, overfly an airbase. To the right is buzz number BM-037, a B-36B-5-CF, while at the center is BM-024, a B-36A-15-CF. Several B-36s are on the ground. **Top right:** B-36s fly low in formation. Early on, defensive doctrine for the B-36 called for the planes to defend themselves with their guns, since they would not have fighter cover on long-range missions. Three-plane formations were specified for optimal fields of fire. (American Aviation Historical Society, two) **Above left:** To expedite the complicated logistics of maintaining the B-36 fleet, pods fabricated from two conjoined engine nacelles and mounted on the bottom of the fuselage of the B-36 were developed for carrying spare engines. The pods were not deployed operationally. (National Museum of the United States Air Force) **Above right:** Five B-36s, including one with an Arctic Red scheme, race along at low altitude. Although the B-36 was designed operate at altitudes above the capability of most enemy fighters, they also were able to conduct bombing runs and operations at low altitudes. (Stan Piet collection)

Top left: What appear to be the same five B-36s seen in the preceding photograph proceed at low altitude above the countryside. During performance tests, the B-36B achieved a top speed of 381 miles per hour and an average cruising speed of 300 miles per hour at 40,000 feet. (Stan Piet collection) **Above left:** During an open house at an airfield, civilians inspect B-36B-5-CF 44-92039. The Eighth Air Force insignia is on the tail, and the recessed tracks for the forward and aft top turret bays are visible to the fronts of the national insignia and the U.S. Air Force inscription. (American Aviation Historical Society **Right:** At least 15 B-36s are visible in this view taken at an unidentified air force base. Several B-36As are present, including BM-013 and BM-025, while BM-029 in the left background and BM-034 are B-36B-1-CFs. Instead of buzz numbers, some planes have the United States Air Force inscription; some have an application of Arctic Red. BM-013 and BM-025 have incomplete Eighth Air Force triangles on their tails, probably due to a swapping of their rudders. (American Aviation Historical Society)

In a U.S. Air Force demonstration, a B-36 leads a formation of various bomber and fighter aircraft: a Boeing B-29 or B-50, a Boeing B-17, a Douglas B-26, and a North American F-51. A display like this could only emphasize the might of the B-36. (National Museum of the United States Air Force)

Left: Cameramen film a passing formation of B-36s flying over what appears to be an airfield. All three planes lack buzz numbers, having instead the nine-inch-tall "UNITED STATES AIR FORCE" inscription on the forward part of the fuselage, barely distinguishable from a distance. The farthest B-36 has the Eighth Air Force insignia on the vertical tail, and the rudder, which has part of that air force's triangular tactical symbol, probably was salvaged from another B-36. (American Aviation Historical Society)

Right: During the inauguration of President Harry Truman on 15 January 1949, a formation of five B-36s of the 7th Bombardment Wing performed several flyovers of the U.S. Capitol during an air review. Four of the planes and the port wingtip of another are present in this view of one of the flyovers. The planes were based at Carswell Air Force Base, Texas. Demonstrations of this type were common on both sides during the Cold War to show off the latest military advances. (Stan Piet collection)

Top left: In an attempt to increase the speed of the B-36, Convair proposed to replace the engines and pusher propellers with six forward-pointing Variable Discharge Turbine (VDT) R-4360-51 Wasp Major engines with tractor propellers. This is a mockup of a nacelle. **Top right:** The designation B-36C was given to the proposed aircraft with VDT engines. On this wooden mockup of a B-36C nacelle, the propeller spinner is to the left.

Between the spinner and the wing is a monocoque section through which the propeller shaft passed. **Above:** A mockup of part of a B-36C wing is viewed from the front. To the left is a partially completed nacelle; spaces for two other nacelles are at the center and the right. The engines were still to be mounted in the same places in the wings, only pointing forward. (National Museum of the United States Air Force, all)

The B-36D

The B-36D marked a significant advance in the B-36 line, with the addition of four General Electric J47-GE-19 turbojet engines (some early B-36Ds employed J47-GE-11 engines) mounted two per pod under each wing, in addition to the six R-4360-41 radial engines. The jet engines provided extra thrust when necessary, such as during takeoff and while taking evasive action, and otherwise were turned off during flight. To test the efficacy of jet engines on the B-36, tests were conducted with B-36B-10-CF serial number 44-92057, seen here during takeoff. (American Aviation Historical Society)

Top left: The GE J47 turbojet engine used in the B-36D and later models was first flight-tested in 1948. It was 144 inches long, 39.5 inches in diameter, and weighed 2,707 pounds. Main components were a 12-stage axial compressor and a single-stage axial turbine. (National Museum of the United States Air Force) **Top right:** The inner components of a General Electric J47 turbojet engine are displayed in cutaway form with a Plexiglas enclosure. The engine air intake is to the left, followed, left to right, by the 12-stage axial compressor, the combustion stage, and the exhaust. (National Museum of the United States Air Force) **Above:** Built as B-36B-10-CF serial number 44-92057, this aircraft was used as the proof-of-concept aircraft for mounting four jet engines on a B-36. This plane was not considered a B-36D conversion until later in its career, when it received full D-model features. (American Aviation Historical Society)

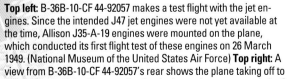

Top left: B-36B-10-CF 44-92057 makes a test flight with the jet engines. Since the intended J47 jet engines were not yet available at the time, Allison J35-A-19 engines were mounted on the plane, which conducted its first flight test of these engines on 26 March 1949. (National Museum of the United States Air Force) **Top right:** A view from B-36B-10-CF 44-92057's rear shows the plane taking off to test the jet engines. The nacelles for the jet engines were made by Convair but were not identical to those used on production B-36Ds, and they also lacked braces on the inboard sides. (American Aviation Historical Society) **Above left:** In addition to B-36Ds built as such, the Air Force decided to convert all of the B-36Bs to B-36Ds by adding J47 engines and installing other D-model features. Conversion work on the B-36Bs was con-

ducted outdoors at Convairs San Diego plant, as seen here. (San Diego Air and Space Museum) **Above right:** Work to turn B-36Bs into B-36Ds is underway at San Diego in 1950. The outer portions of the wings have been removed, and the first two aircraft have Eighth Air Force insignia. The FW and SD codes indicated each plane's original and conversion sequence number. (National Museum of the United States Air Force)

Top: B-36B-1-CF 44-92037 of the 42nd Bombardment Wing had been converted to a B-36D by the time this photo was taken. The propeller spinners, the stripe near the top of the horizontal tail, the nose-wheel doors, and the fronts of the jet engine pods were yellow. **Above:** The same B-36D seen in the preceding photo is viewed from the front while it warms its engines. The diagonal brace used to stabilize the jet engine nacelle is visible on the inboard side of the nacelle. These jet engines used standard aviation fuel, not jet fuel. (Stan Piet collection, both)

Top: Another B-36B converted to a B-36D was serial number 44-92074. It was built as a B-36B-15-CF, was accepted by the U.S. Air Force in July 1949, and at the time it was scrapped in fiscal year 1957, had been modified to B-36D-45-CF-II standards. (National Museum of the United States Air Force)

Above: B-36D-45-CF serial number 44-92074 is viewed from a slightly different angle as it cruises over mountainous terrain. It had few markings, but one of them, the black 71 applied to the nose, represented the plane's Convair construction-sequence number. (National Museum of the United States Air Force)

A close examination of the tail number of this B-36D suggests that the plane was serial number 44-92064, a converted B-36B. A protective cover is secured over the clear nose and cockpit canopy, although the two 20mm cannons of the nose turret are protruding. (Stan Piett collection)

Ground crewmen are rolling a boarding ladder up to B-36D-45-CF serial number 44-92068, a converted B-36B-15-CF. A clear view is provided of the outboard sides of the port jet-engine nacelle and its pylon. Two static dischargers are on the aileron. (American Aviation Historical Society)

Maintenance personnel pore over B-36D-30-CF serial number 49-2036, originally a B-36B-1-CF. On the B-36D, the original track-mounted bomb-bay doors were replaced by quick-operating, snap-action or clamshell doors. Two pairs of doors were fitted to bomb bays one and two and two pairs of doors were fitted to bomb bays three and four. The port door of the two forward bomb bays is visible in the open position. In the left background are maintenance docks, which made the tasks of working on B-36s more convenient. (American Aviation Historical Society)

The considerable size of the B-36 is apparent in this view with the massive bomber in the background, with a Boeing B-50 and B-47, themselves large aircraft, ahead of its wings. Directly ahead of the B-36 is a B-45, with an F-84 Thunderjet in the foreground. This photo summarizes the USAF's transition from a propeller to a jet-powered fighting force. (Stan Piet collection)

A crowd at an air-base open house gather around B-36D-10-CF serial number 44-9026, which, coincidentally, had been converted to model-D standards from the first B-36B. Emblazoned on the nose is the emblem of the 7th Bombardment Wing with its "mors ab alto" motto underneath. On the tail are the triangle-J tactical symbol and the Eighth Air Force insignia. The tip of the vertical tail was painted yellow. The last three digits of the serial number, 026, are marked on the fuselage below the "United States Air Force" inscription. (Stan Piet collection)

Convair B-36D-45-CF serial number 44-92080 was photographed on the runway at San Diego soon after its conversion from a B-36B-20-CF to a D-model. This bomber was redelivered to the U.S. Air Force in the latter part of 1951 and was assigned to the 92nd Bombardment Wing. The aircraft did not enjoy a long career as a B-36D: on 29 January 1952, it landed short and crashed while approaching Fairchild Air Force Base, near Spokane, Washington. Although the crewmen all survived, the bomber was written off. (Stan Piet collection)

In addition to the in-service B-36Bs converted to B-36Ds, 26 B-36s, serials 44-92095 to 44-92098 and 49-2647 to 49-2668, were built as D models, including four originally started as B-36Bs but converted to B-36Ds on Convair's assembly line. Seen here during a flight is the first as-built D model, B-36D-1-CDF serial number 44-92095, which was delivered to the U.S. Air Force in April 1950. This plane was one of the four B-36Ds originally ordered as a B-36B. It was employed in testing the E-5 autopilot system. (National Museum of the United States Air Force)

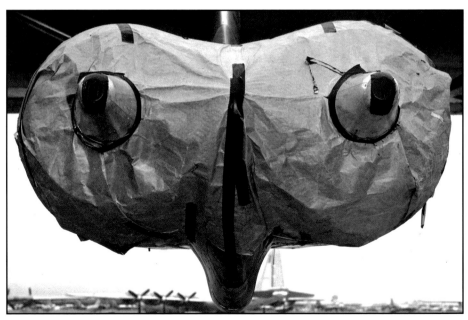

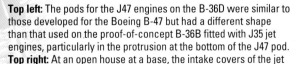

Top left: The pods for the J47 engines on the B-36D were similar to those developed for the Boeing B-47 but had a different shape than that used on the proof-of-concept B-36B fitted with J35 jet engines, particularly in the protrusion at the bottom of the J47 pod.
Top right: At an open house at a base, the intake covers of the jet engines, seen in the open position in the preceding photo, are closed. These covers were closed when the engines were not in use during flight, but they allowed enough air to slip by to rotate the compressor. **Above left:** The closed intake covers of the starboard J47 jet engines are viewed from the front. On the front of the protrusion at the lower center of the engine pod is a landing light, set behind a contoured clear cover. A similar landing light was on the port pod as well. **Above right:** A fabric cover has been fitted over the intakes of the J47 jet engines to keep out foreign objects and moisture. The compressor spinners protrude through the cover, and what appears to be black tape has been applied over the openings at the fronts of the spinners. (San Diego Air and Space Museum, all)

B-36D-5-CF 49-2648 is viewed from below the engine nacelles of another B-36. Curiously, twin radomes are present over the tail turret, probably representing a retrofitted AN/APG-41 radar installation, a type introduced with the B-36H. (American Aviation Historical Society)

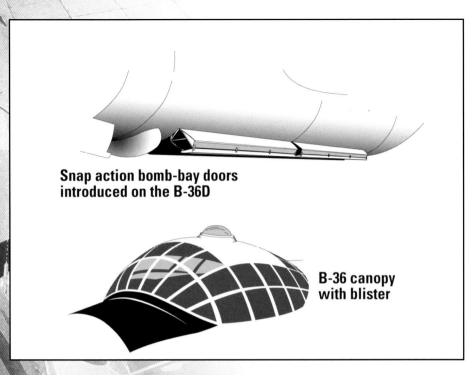

Snap action bomb-bay doors
introduced on the B-36D

B-36 canopy
with blister

Top left: Two key features that differentiated the B-36D from the B-36B are illustrated: the change from sliding bomb-bay doors on each bomb bay to fast-acting, snap-action doors, each set covering two bomb bays; and the addition of an astrodome to the D-model canopy. **Top right:** Convair B-36D-5-CF serial number 49-2652 was named *Pretty Girl*; the name is inscribed below the cockpit. The plane was accepted by the U.S. Air Force in August 1950. On the vertical tail is the triangle-J sign of the 7th Bombardment Wing (Heavy). (National Museum of the United States Air Force) **Above:** B-36D-1-CF 44-92098 was the last of the four D-model planes originally ordered as a B-36B under contract number AF33-038-AC7. A fabric cover is fitted over the gunner's dome aft of the cockpit canopy, and the plane is tied down to prevent wind damage. (American Aviation Historical Society)

Top: On 15 October 1951, B-36D-35-CF 49-2664 of the 436th Bomb Squadron, 7th Bomb Wing, suffered a main landing gear failure at Kirtland Air Force Base, New Mexico. Damage was minimal, and this was the only B-36 to be returned to service after crashing. **Above:** Ill-fated B-36D-25-CF 49-2658 of the 436th Bomb Squadron, 7th Bomb Wing, Carswell Air Force Base, Texas, collided with an F-51D-25-NT Mustang during gunnery training over Oklahoma on 27 April 1951, killing the Mustang pilot and 13 of 17 B-36 crewmen. (American Aviation Historical Society, both)

Top left: Convair B-36D-1-CF serial number 44-92096 was one of the four B-36Ds originally ordered as a B-36B. At the bottom of the fuselage are three radomes for ferret electronic countermeasures antennas, a feature normally found on RB-36 reconnaissance bombers. (American Aviation Historical Society) **Top right:** This aircraft appears to have been one of the two proof-of concept aircraft that tested the jet-engine installation on B-36Bs, and not a B-36D, because tracks are on the side of the fuselage for the sliding-type bomb-bay doors, whereas B-36Ds had snap-action doors. **Above:** B-36D-1-CF serial number 44-92096 cruises among the clouds above an arid landscape. At the bottom of the fuselage forward of the wings are two masts with a wire antenna between them; this was a marker-beacon antenna for the instrument-landing system. (American Aviation Historical Society)

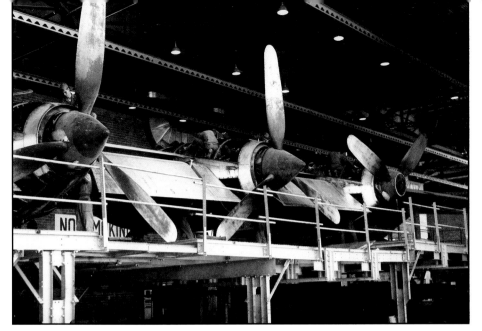

Top left: The starboard wing of a B-36 is positioned above an all-weather maintenance dock that Convair constructed. This dock is a stationary type; a portable type also was developed. Most B-36 facilities, including Convair's San Antonio plant, had maintenance docks. (American Aviation Historical Society) **Top right:** A B-36, apparently a D model from what can be discerned of the tail number, and another B-36 in the background are undergoing maintenance on Okinawa. The man on the work platform is making adjustments to the twin 20mm cannons of the tail turret. Above the cannons are twin radomes used in the aiming of the tail turret, likely a retrofit, as stock B-36Ds as built had a single radome in that position. On the wings, men are working on the engines. (Stan Piet collection) **Above:** Two of the 92nd Bomb Wing's B-36s are undergoing maintenance work on Okinawa. The top turret bays of the nearer bomber are open. The first four digits of that plane's tail number appear to be 9264, which would indicate that this was a B-36D-5-CF. (American Aviation Historical Society)

Ten B-36s of the 92nd Bomb Wing, including three in the foreground, one in the center background, and six in the left background, are at a base on Okinawa on 25 August 1953. The planes were on a 30-day deployment on orders of President Dwight D. Eisenhower. (American Aviation Historical Society)

The RB-36D

Because of the B-36's long range and its ability to fly at high altitudes, the Air Force decided to acquire a reconnaissance version of the bomber, the RB-36. The first sub-model was the RB-36D, based on the B-36D. These reconnaissance aircraft were equipped with an array of photographic equipment, ferret electronic countermeasures (FECM) equipment, and the full defensive armaments suite. All 24 of the RB-36Ds were delivered to the 28th Strategic Reconnaissance Wing (Heavy), based at Rapid City Air Force Base, South Dakota. (National Museum of the United States Air Force)

The trolley for elevating the front of the plane for the rollout from the factory is being fitted under an RB-36D. The forward bomb-bay fuselage section with its dull magnesium skin had been replaced by a pressurized camera compartment with shiny aluminum skin. (National Museum of the United States Air Force)

Two RB-36Ds assigned to the 28th Strategic Reconnaissance Wing (Heavy), including 49-2688, an RB-36D-10-CF, in the foreground, cruise low over badlands. Three FECM radomes are under the fuselages; FECM equipment was housed in former bomb bay four. (National Museum of the United States Air Force)

The tail number is illegible on this RB-36, probably a D model. The U.S. Air Force inscription on the side of the fuselage is the late type, with 36-inch-high letters, which replaced the earlier, 9-inch-tall letters on B-36s and RB-36s around late 1955. (American Aviation Historical Society)

Top: Though the tail number is indistinct on this RB-36D, it appears to be 92686, which would represent serial number 49-2686, the first RB-36D, delivered in September 1950. On the tail is the triangle-S tactical sign of the 28th Strategic Reconnaissance Wing (Heavy). (National Museum of the United States Air Force)

Above: Civilians inspect RB-36D-15-CF 49-2694. Although all RB-36s were built with the FECM radomes below former bomb bay four, these radomes had been relocated aft as part of a modification to restore bomb bay four for use in carrying nuclear weapons. (American Aviation Historical Society)

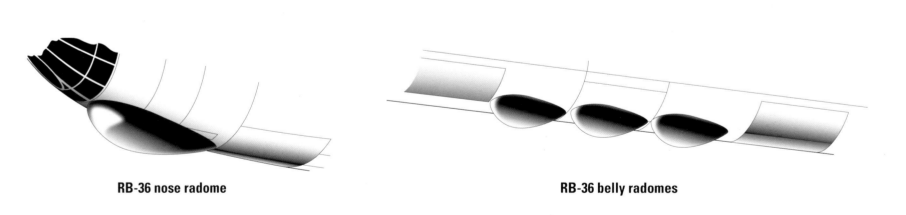

RB-36 nose radome

RB-36 belly radomes

Top: Convair RB-36D-15-CF 49-2694 is observed from a different angle. This plane later was converted to a GRB-36D-15-CF-III for use as a carrier aircraft in experiments to enable B-36s and RB-36s to carry parasite fighters and recon planes on operational missions. **Above:** Unlike B-36s, RB-36s had a radome containing defensive ECM and ferret ECM antennas in the chin position. RB-36s also were built with three FECM radomes below the former location of bomb bay four, although later they were moved aft as a modification.

The RB-36E

The Convair RB-36E comprised remanufactured B-36As as well as YB-36 42-13571, and this model was powered by Pratt & Whitney R-4360-25 Wasp Major radial engines and J47-GE-19 turbojet engines. Snap-action bomb-bay doors were installed. In most other respects, the RB-36E was similar to the RB-36D. Seen here is RB-36E-10-CF 44-92020, which was converted from a B-36A-15-CF. (National Museum of the United States Air Force)

Top left: Convair mechanics at the Fort Worth plant are conducting rebuilding work to transform a B-36A into an RB-36E. The R-4360 radial engines and the flaps have been removed from the port wing, and cribbing is being constructed to support the fuselage. **Top right:** During the remanufacturing process for the RB-36E, the fuselage forward of the wings was removed and stored on a stand. Later, this part of the fuselage would be grafted onto a new section of fuselage that contained a pressurized camera compartment. **Above left:** The forward fuselage of B-36A 44-92016 is supported by a trolley and is in the process of being detached from the plane on 18 July 1950. Jack stands support the wings. The radome has been detached from aft of the nose landing gear bay and is on the tarmac. **Above right:** Workmen operate on the forward pressurized section of fuselage from B-36A-10-CF 44-92016 during the rebuilding of the plane into a RB-36E. Protective film has been applied to the cockpit canopy, the gunner's sighting dome, and the bombardier's clear nose.

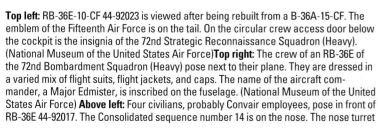

Top left: RB-36E-10-CF 44-92023 is viewed after being rebuilt from a B-36A-15-CF. The emblem of the Fifteenth Air Force is on the tail. On the circular crew access door below the cockpit is the insignia of the 72nd Strategic Reconnaissance Squadron (Heavy). (National Museum of the United States Air Force) **Top right:** The crew of an RB-36E of the 72nd Bombardment Squadron (Heavy) pose next to their plane. They are dressed in a varied mix of flight suits, flight jackets, and caps. The name of the aircraft commander, a Major Edmister, is inscribed on the fuselage. (National Museum of the United States Air Force) **Above left:** Four civilians, probably Convair employees, pose in front of RB-36E 44-92017. The Consolidated sequence number 14 is on the nose. The nose turret has been removed and the opening covered over. Four ECM antennas are on the fuselage aft of the four men. **Above right:** The forward top turret bay doors are open and the starboard turret is visible in the raised position on RB-36E-5-CF serial number 44-92012 as the engines are being warmed. The last three digits of the serial number are painted in large figures on the fuselage. (National Archives)

85

The B-36F

Two B-36F-5-CFs, serial numbers 49-2682 in the foreground and 49-2680 in the distance, fly in formation. The insignias on the forward part of the fuselages are the pirate-in-a-triangle design of the 6th Bombardment Wing (Heavy). Fourteen B-36Fs were delivered to the U.S. Air Force. They were similar to the preceding model, the B-36D, but had more powerful R-4360-53 radial engines, rated at 3,800 horsepower, resulting in a higher maximum speed, 413 miles per hour, and a higher service ceiling, 44,000 feet. (American Aviation Historical Society)

Top left: On the nose of B-36F-5-CF serial number 49-2683 is Convair sequence number 164: a sequence number was assigned to B-36s and RB-36s starting with the first B-36A. At the front of the antiglare panel in front of the cockpit is an antenna for the blind-approach set. **Top right:** Convair B-36F-5-CF serial number 49-2683 is observed from the forward starboard quarter. Early B-36Fs featured the new 2CFR87C-1 fire-control system for its defensive weapons, but starting with 50-1064 the improved 2CFR87C-2 system was installed. **Above left:** In 1957 B-36F-1-CF 49-2677 ferried a structural test article comprising an incomplete B-58 bomber from Fort Worth to Wright-Patterson Air Force Base in Ohio. The B-36F had its inboard propellers removed, and the landing gear was extended for the entire flight. **Above right:** Two B-36s, including B-36F-5-CF serial number 49-2683 in the foreground, fly in formation. Both planes have anti-thermal white paint on their undersides and the 36-inch-high letters for the "United States Air Force" markings on the fuselage sides. (American Aviation Historical Society, all)

Convair B-36F-5-CF serial number 49-2680 of the 6th Bombardment Wing (Heavy) is viewed from the starboard beam in flight. The pirate-in-a-triangle insignia of the bomb wing is applied to the fuselage forward of the cockpit. The last three digits of the serial number are marked forward of the "United States Air Force" inscription on the fuselage. The border at the top of the anti-thermal white paint on the fuselage had an angled jog just forward of the national insignia. (American Aviation Historical Society)

Top left: B-36F-1-CF 49-2677 flies with the B-58 structural test article slung underneath in 1957. At Wright-Patterson Air Force Base, Ohio, the test article would undergo static stress tests until it was destroyed, in order to calculate the B-58's structural strength. (National Museum of the United States Air Force) **Top right:** The B-36F-1-CF carrier airplane with the B-58 structural test article is viewed from another angle while coming in for the landing at Wright-Patterson Air Force Base. The test article lacked the engine installations, nose cone, and other standard assemblies. (American Aviation Historical Society) **Above left:** In a view of B-36F-1-CF 49-2677 ferrying the B-58 structural test article, the big bomber's main landing gear wheels are about to touch down on the runway. The lack of the inboard propellers is evident; they were removed to provide clearance for the B-58. (American Aviation Historical Society) **Above right:** The B-36F carrier aircraft and its cargo of the B-58 structural test article are on the ground. This photo and the preceding ones are graphic evidence of the large disparity in size between the B-36 and the B-58, soon to become operational a supersonic bomber. (National Museum of the United States Air Force)

The RB-36F

B-36 Comparison

	XB-36	B-36B	B-36D	RB-36F	B-36J
Armament:	none	16 x 20mm M24A1	16 x 20mm M24A1	16 x 20mm M24A1	2 x 20mm M24A1
Bomb Load	72,000 lbs.	86,000 lbs.	86,000 lbs.	86,000 lbs.	86,000 lbs.
Engines:	6 x Pratt & Whitney R-4360-25	6 x Pratt & Whitney R-4360-41	6 x Pratt & Whitney R-4360-41 + 4 x GE J47-19 turbojet	6 x Pratt & Whitney R-4360-53 + 4 x GE J47-19 turbojet	6 x Pratt & Whitney R-4360-53 + 4 x GE J47-19 turbojet
Horsepower/thrust	3,000 hp each (takeoff power)	3,500 hp max each	3,500 hp + 5,200 lbs. thrust max each	3,500 hp + 5,200 lbs. thrust max each	3,500 hp + 5,200 lbs. thrust max each
Maximum speed:	346 mph at 35,000 ft.	381 mph @ 34,500 ft.	439 mph @ 32,120 ft.	417 @ 37,100 ft.	411 @ 36,400 ft.
Cruising speed:	216 mph	202 mph	225 mph	235 mph	203 mph
Range:	9,500 miles with 10,000 lbs. bomb load 8,175 miles	7,500 miles	7,743 miles	6,800 miles	
Service ceiling:	36,000 ft.	42,000 ft.	45,200 ft.	44,000 ft.	39,900 ft.
Span:	230 ft. 0 in.	230 ft. 0 in.	230 ft. 0 in.	230 ft. 0 in	230 ft. 0 in
Length:	162 ft. 1 in.	162 ft. 1 in.	162 ft. 1 in.	162 ft. 1 in.	162 ft. 1 in.
Height:	46 ft. 8 in.	46 ft. 8 in.	46 ft. 8 in.	46 ft. 8 in.	46 ft. 8 in.
Weight:	276,506 lbs. (max. gross weight)	311,000 lbs. (max. gross weight)	370,000 lbs. (max. gross weight)	370,000 lbs. (max. gross weight)	410,000 lbs. (max. gross weight)

Top left: The 24 Convair RB-36Fs delivered to the Air Force had air frames equivalent to those of the B-36F, and their reconnaissance equipment was similar to that of the RB-36D. Illustrated here is a multi-camera installation as mounted in the RB-36F (National Museum of the United States Air Force). **Top right:** Four flight crewmen officers confer next to RB-36F-5-CF serial number 49-2713. The barrels of the 20mm cannons in the nose turrets have sleeve-type protective covers over them. The last four digits of the plane's serial number are stenciled on the nose-gear door. (Stan Piet collection)

Above left: Ground crewmen perform maintenance work on an RB-36F. In the foreground, one of them makes adjustments to the top of the rudder. Below and to the front of the rudder, the aft top gun-turret bay is open, with the turrets visible inside. On the port wing, panels of the engine nacelles have been removed, and mechanics are working on the Pratt & Whitney R-4360-53 Wasp Major radial engines. (National Museum of the United States Air Force). **Above right:** A special portable work stand has been set up for ground crewmen to perform work on the rudder of Convair RB-36F-1-CF serial number 49-2704. With its several tiers of platforms fitted with guard rails, a ladder, and a hoist on top, this stand solved the problem of how to work on the tall vertical tail and rudder of the B-36s and RB-36s. On the vertical fin is the insignia of the Fifteenth Air Force. (Stan Piet collection)

The GRB-36F

In a continuing attempt to devise means for B-36s to ferry their own parasite fighter or reconnaissance aircraft with them on long-range missions, the Fighter Conveyor (FICON) project developed a bomb-bay-mounted trapeze docking system to allow the fighter to launch from and dock to the bomber in flight. Convair RB-36F serial number 49-2707 was selected as the carrier aircraft for the experiment and was redesignated the GRB-36F. Here, Republic EF-84E-1-RE Thunderjet 49-2115 maneuvers up to the trapeze to achieve a connection before being retracted to the belly of the bomber in early 1952. (American Aviation Historical Society)

Top left: Republic EF-84E-1-RE Thunderjet serial number 49-2115 has trapped the front of the boom of the trapeze of JRB-36F serial number 49-2707. The next step would be the locking of the parasite plane to two latches extending below the bottom of the boom. **Top right:** The EF-84E is locked to the trapeze of the GRB-36F. The next step in the procedure was intended to be the hoisting of the parasite plane to the belly of the carrier. However, the first two attempts to dock the parasite failed because of instability in the trapeze. **Above left:** The GRB-36F included a trapeze operator's station in the rear of the camera compartment. The operator sat facing aft and could see the trapeze and the parasite fighter through the bomb bay using the window at the lower left. Control panels are around the window. (American Aviation Historical Society) **Above right:** Republic RF-84K 52-7269 is attached to the trapeze. Having the RF-84K as a parasite plane gave the carrier the ability to launch a fast reconnaissance plane to make a dash into enemy territory while the more vulnerable carrier stood off at a safe range.

At Fairchild Air Force Base, Washington, the parasite fighter was lowered into a specially constructed pit in order to mount it on the trapeze of the carrier plane before takeoff. Then the carrier plane was moved over the pit and the loading was commenced. (Stan Piet collection)

Top left: When the parasite plane was retracted to the carrier, as seen here, the cockpit canopy protruded into the bomb bay so the pilot could enter or exit his plane. Once the parasite plane was launched and the trapeze gear was retracted, plug doors covered the opening. (American Aviation Historical Society) **Top right:** An RF-84K is mounted on the trapeze of the carrier prior to takeoff. Very little ground clearance was beneath the parasite aircraft. The horizontal stabilizers/elevators of the RF-84F had a pronounced anhedral (downward cant) to allow clearance with the bomb bay. (Stan Piet collection)

Above: Ten RB-36Ds were converted to GRB-36D-III FICON operational carriers in the mid-1950s. Here, GRB-36D-III 49-2694 has an RF-84 slung underneath. The GRB-36D-IIIs were assigned to the 99th Strategic Reconnaissance Wing at Fairchild Air Force Base. (American Aviation Historical Society)

Top: Atop the fuselage of GRB-36D-III 49-2694 above the "U.S." part of the "U.S. Air Force" inscription is the distinctive dome for the antenna of the AN-APX-29A UFF/rendezvous set, which allowed the parasite aircraft to establish the location of the carrier plane. (American Aviation Historical Society) **Above left:** Republic YF-84F serial number 49-2430 was developed as a FICON parasite fighter plane. On top of the front of the fuselage is the "duck bill" docking probe. The names "Christine" with an X through it and "George" are painted on the side of the fuselage **Above right:** YF-84F 49-2430 is viewed from the starboard side. This aircraft began as an F-84E before being modified to a YF-84F parasite fighter. This aircraft is now on display at the National Museum of the United States Air Force, Wright-Patterson Air Force Base.

Top left: As a chase plane flies alongside, YF-84F serial number 49-2430 has made contact with the boom of the JRB-36F, and soon two latches to either side of the main jack of the trapeze will lock onto the parasite plane, firmly securing it to the boom.**Top right:** The probe atop the nose of the YF-84F has been captured by the boom, establishing the first step in the linking process. Next, latches on the two extensions on the bottom of the boom will be locked to pins mounted on each side of the fuselage of the YF-84F.
Above left: The YF-84F parasite plane has been captured by the trapeze of the JRB-36F and has been retracted to the bottom of the carrier plane. It can be seen why it was necessary to revamp the parasite plane's elevators/horizontal stabilizers to allow the plane to fit in the bay. **Above right:** Much of the parasite aircraft was exposed below the belly of the GRB-36F carrier plane when docked to the carrier. The space between the bay and the parasite was not sealed on the GRB-36F but would be sealed by special doors on the production GRB-36D.

The pilot of YF-84F 49-2430 cautiously maneuvers his plane toward the boom of the JRB-36F carrier plane, serial number 49-2707. The boom was suspended from a snubber at the front, a main jack aft of center, and a two-legged drag strut at the rear. (National Museum of the United States Air Force)

The B-36H

B-36H-50-CH serial number 52-1350 takes off, landing gear still extended. The B-36H was the most numerous model of the B-36, with a production run of 83 aircraft. In outward appearances it was similar to the B-36F. Most changes were internal, including the relocation of the K-system ECM equipment into a pressurized compartment; a remodeled flight deck with a station for a second flight engineer, and improved illumination in the crew compartments. Partway through B-36H production, the single tail-turret radome was replaced by a twin-radome installation. (American Aviation Historical Society)

Top left: A B-36H is under construction at Convair's plant in Fort Worth, Texas. Wide variations in color tones of the various skin panels of the wings and fuselage are evident. Lying on a pallet on the factory floor toward the center of the photo are two main-landing gear struts. **Top right:** Convair technicians make adjustments to General Electric J47-GE-19 turbojet engines mounted under a starboard wing. The intake covers on these engines are in the extended, or "closed," position. The engine brace is visible behind the man on top of the engine. **Above:** B-36H-1-CF serial number 50-1085 exhibits the 36-inch-high "United States Air Force" fuselage markings introduced around late 1955. This aircraft was redesignated an EDB-36H-1-CF and used in nuclear-weapons testing before being scrapped in December 1956. (American Aviation Historical Society)

Left: A series of three Featherweight conversion projects was implemented to lighten B-36s and RB-36s. This plane appears to have undergone Featherweight III modifications, in which, among other measures, all of the gun turrets except the tail turret were removed. To the starboard of the center of the clear nose, the opening for the turret sight has been covered, and the bombardier's optically flat aiming window has been covered, since the plane was fitted with a periscopic bomb sight. **Right:** For the B-36H, a new propeller was introduced, designated a high-altitude propeller since it operated more efficiently at great altitude. The blades had a wider chord and less pitch than the original propeller blades and were fabricated by a flash-welding procedure. The most noticeable change from the earlier propeller was the squared tips of the blades. The high-altitude propellers were installed on B-36Hs during construction and were retrofitted on most earlier models of B-36s and RB-36s. (American Aviation Historical Society, both)

Top left: A Pratt & Whitney R-4360 engine assembly is being delivered to an aircraft. The assembly included the engine, cowling, and mounting fixtures. The assembly was nicknamed the "power egg," and it made for relatively fast engine changes. **Top right:** B-36H-50-CH 52-1350 takes off on a flight. The landing gear is midway through the re-traction process, with the main gear swinging upward and inboard. Of interest is the lack of national insignia on the side of the fuselage and the bottoms of the wings. **Above:** Civilians get a look at B-36H 50-1092 at an air show at Detroit on 1 September 1952. On the side of the nose is the insignia of the 11th Bombardment Group (Heavy), and on the tail are the triangle-U tactical sign of that bomb group and the Eighth Air Force emblem. (American Aviation Historical Society, all)

A few B-36Hs, including EB-36H-35-CF serial number 51-5731 here, were converted to EB-36Hs for use in nuclear-weapons tests. The insignia below the cockpit was that of the 4925th Test Group (Atomic), based at Kirtland Air Force Base, New Mexico. (Stan Piet collection)

Top left: The port side of the forward part of the fuselage of EB-36H-30-CF serial number 51-5726A is seen close-up, providing a view of the insignia of the 4925th Test Group (Atomic). The 20mm cannons have been dismounted from the nose turret. (Stan Piet collection) **Top right:** The EB-36H-30-CF shown in the preceding photos was repainted in a unique red, white, blue, and black paint scheme while used as a high-altitude "target" craft at the Atlantic Missile Range, Florida. The scheme facilitated calibrating ground-based cameras. **Above:** EB-36H-30-CF 51-5726A is observed from the forward starboard quarter. After 1955, this aircraft was redesignated a JB-36H. The Air Force used several modified B-36s to drop real and simulated bombs and test the effects of nuclear blasts on the B-36. (Stan Piet collection)

The NB-36H

The Convair NB-36H Crusader, seen here with a B-50 chase plane, was an experimental version of the B-36 intended to test radioactive shielding for a five-man crew compartment in a nuclear-powered aircraft. For this purpose, the NB-36H had onboard a small, functioning nuclear reactor, but the reactor was not connected to the plane's propulsion system. The NB-36H also was referred to as the Nuclear Test Aircraft (NTA), and the basic plane was B-36H-20-CF, serial number 51-5712, which had been severely damaged by a tornado that struck Carswell Air Force Base on 1 September 1952.

Top left: General Electric conducted a series of Heat Transfer Reactor Experiments (HTRE) at the Idaho National Laboratory in the 1950s to test the concept of operating a J47 jet engine by nuclear power. Here is the reactor used in the third stage of the experiment, HTRE-3. (National Museum of the United States Air Force

Top right: The NB-36H wore on its tail the international symbol for radioactivity, a trefoil inside a circle, which was introduced in 1946. To the front of the national insignia on the fuselage is an air scoop for the reactor's cooling system; a similar scoop was on the other side. (National Museum of the United States Air Force)

Above left: The front of the fuselage of the NB-36 was a completely new design, which enclosed a heavily shielded crew compartment for five men to protect them from the radioactivity of the reactor. The windshield comprised six-inch-thick Plexiglas of high optical clarity. (National Museum of the United States Air Force) **Above right:** The NB-36 had more decorative paint touches than the average B-36, with red on the fronts of the jet engine nacelles and the reactor air scoops, a wide blue cheat line with a narrower red cheat line below it, and, apparently, green on the top of the vertical tail.

Top left: The NB-36H generates contrails as it cruises at high altitude during a test flight. Because of the thickness of the shielding of the crew compartment, the compartment was quite cramped. The aircraft was designed to allow the removal of the crew compartment. (National Museum of the United States Air Force) **Above left:** The Atomic Energy Commission collaborated with Convair and the U.S. Air Force to design and produce the NB-36H, and the round, light-colored shape overlapping the cheat line to the front of the wing is the insignia of the Atomic Energy Commission. **Right:** The reactor carried aboard the NB-36H was designated the Aircraft Shield Test Reactor (ASTR). It is shown being hoisted into its position in bomb bay four of the NB-36H. The ASTR was a 1,000-kilowatt, air-cooled unit weighing 35,000 pounds. Visible here are the right side and the rear of the ASTR. On the rear of the unit is a maze of moderator inlet and outlet lines, connections, ion chambers, and gamma monitor, and a structure called the cow's tail.

The RB-36H

The U.S. Air Force acquired 73 RB-36Hs, a reconnaissance model based on the B-36H. Photographic and ferret electronic countermeasures equipment on the RB-36H was similar to that carried on preceding versions of the RB-36. Here, the forward top turrets are deployed on RB-36H serial number 51-13739. Clear details of other features on the front of the fuselage also are visible, including the radome aft of the nose landing gear, the circular access hatch below the cockpit, and the antenna installations. (National Museum of the United States Air Force)

Above left: In the RB-36H, several crewmen were stationed in the nose compartment, including the radar-navigator on the port side, the radar-observer on the starboard side, and a photo-navigator. These quarters were quite cramped, as seen here facing forward. (Stan Piet collection) **Right:** As was the case in other B-36s and RB-36s, the radio operator's compartment in the RB-36H was on the lower level just aft of the flight deck. Here, the radio operator has his right hand on the telegraph key of his radio transmitter. To the upper right is a gun sighting station, including a gun sight and clear Plexiglas dome. The radio operator is wearing a parachute harness and pack. (Stan Piet collection) **Top left:** The 20mm cannon turrets are extended on this RB-36H, including the top aft turrets and, directly below them, the two belly turrets. Also in view are the open doors of bomb bay four and aft of them, the three ferret electronic countermeasures antenna domes. (National Museum of the United States Air Force)

Top: The U.S. Air Force accepted RB-36H-55-CH serial number 52-1382 in June 1953. On the chin of the fuselage aft of the clear nose is a blister containing antenna equipment for defensive electronic countermeasures and low-frequency electronic countermeasures. (American Aviation Historical Society) **Above:** Streaming contrails, this RB-36H shows off the white underside paint that was characteristic of the so-called high altitude camouflage paint. It was hoped that the white paint would protect sensitive areas of the bomber from heat flash from an atomic weapons blast. (National Museum of the United States Air Force)

The B-36J

The B-36J was the last production model of the B-36, of which 33 examples were produced. The maiden flight of the B-36J was on 3 September 1953, and the last one was rolled out on 14 August 1954. It differed from the B-36H principally in that it had an extra fuel tank with a capacity of 1,385 gallons toward the outer part of each wing, and its landing gear was reinforced. The final 14 B-36Js left the assembly line as Featherweight III aircraft, with all turrets except the tail one deleted. Seen here is B-36J-1-CF 52-2217. (Stan Piet collection)

Top: A B-36J takes off. The underside of the plane has an anti-thermal white paint designed to offer some defense against the heat pulse of a nuclear explosion. The difference in sheen between the aluminum- and magnesium-skinned areas of the fuselage is apparent. (National Museum of the United States Air Force)

Above: B-36J-10-CF-III 52-2820 was accepted by the Air Force in June 1954. The III in the plane's designation stood for the Featherweight III standards, the third in the series of programs to reduce the weight of the B-36s by removing weapons and nonessential items. (American Aviation Historical Society)

Top left: The three black cars parked next to Convair B-36J-10-CF-III serial number 52-2825, the presence of a movie camera and operator, and the officer shaking hands with a crewmember at the bottom of the stairs indicate that a special occasion was underway. (American Aviation Historical Society) **Top right:** To commemorate the final Peacemaker produced, the plane, B-36J-10-CF USAF serial number 52-2827, was assigned the nickname "Dear John," and a placard was affixed to the fuselage for Convair workers to sign. The script at the top of the placard reads, "Dear John / how I hate to see you go / Signed." **Above left:** Starting with B-36H-40-CF serial number 51-5742, the AN/APG-41 fire-control radar was installed in the Peacemakers. As seen here, this radar featured two side-by-side radomes. Some Peacemakers fitted with this radar later had a single, wide radome to replace the two separate radomes. (National Museum of the United States Air Force) **Above right:** B-36J-1-CF 52-2220 had the honor of making the last flight ever flown by a B-36, when it flew from Davis-Monthan Air Force Base in Arizona to Wright Field in Ohio to be donated to the Air Force Museum. In this photo, the plane is in deteriorated condition. (National Museum of the United States Air Force)

The YB-60

Convair developed the YB-60, an all-jet, swept-wing bomber, without the benefit of receiving a government contract for it. Convair intended the plane as a potential stop-gap should the Boeing B-52, slated to replace the B-36 as a strategic bomber, suffer extended developmental problems or cancellation. The YB-60 took a basic B-36 fuse-lage and added a redesigned, streamlined nose, and swept wings fashioned by re-modeling the stock wings. Eight Pratt & Whitney YJ57-P-3 turbojet engines were mounted under the wings in four pods. Two YB-60s were built, but only the first one ever flew, as seen here. The prototypes were assigned serial numbers 49-2676 and 49-2684; the latter was almost completed but was never flown. (Stan Piet collection)

The first YB-60, shown during construction inside the Hangar Building at Convair's Fort Worth plant, was fitted with a detachable nose with a flight-test boom. Previously, a different, production-type nose without a boom had been fitted on this aircraft. (National Museum of the United States Air Force)

Top left: The front of the fuselage of the first YB-60 has been elevated on a trolley so the top of the vertical tail will fit under the Hangar Building's door for the roll-out. The YJ57-P-3 engines were in short supply, and the last of them was installed just before roll-out. (San Diego Air and Space Museum) **Top right:** The first YB-60 is viewed from the rear at the time of its roll-out, the bottom of the rear of the fuselage almost touching the floor of the Hangar Building. The main landing gear wheels rested on special trolleys during the roll-out. The rudder was not yet installed. (San Diego Air and Space Museum) **Above left:** The YB-60 had a streamlined tail-turret installation, more conical shaped than the ball-shaped tail-turret shield of the B-36. The tail turret had a single radome containing the two antennas of the APG-42

radar. The snap-action bomb-bay doors are open. (San Diego Air and Space Museum) **Above right:** YB-60 number one rests on a hardstand with three B-36s visible in the background. The cheat line, "Convair YB-60" inscription, and decorative work on the nose were red. The indentation in the antiglare panel marked the rear edge of the detachable nose. (National Museum of the United States Air Force)

Top left: The YB-60 was photographed during its maiden flight on 18 April 1952, with Convair's chief test pilot, Beryl A. Erickson, and copilot Arthur S. Witchell at the controls. During the flight, which lasted 66 minutes, the landing gear was extended the whole time. (National Museum of the United States Air Force) **Top right:** The swept wings of the YB-60 were fabricated by cutting the wings of a B-36 in line with the inboard nacelles, tilting-back the outer sections at an angle of about 38 degrees at the leading edge, and adding a leading-edge "glove" and new leading and trailing edges. (Stan Piet collection) **Above left:** The YB-60 employed YJ-57-P-3 engines, which weighed 4,348 pounds and developed up to 8,700 pounds of thrust under full military power. The engines projected beyond the fronts of the wings to ameliorate a center-of-gravity problem caused by the swept wings. **Above right:** A pint-sized cowboy squares-off against the first YB-60. The fronts of the engine nacelles are fitted with removable covers. On a production B-60, the detachable nose would have housed the K-3A bombing/navigation equipment and radar antenna. (US Air Force)

An overhead view of the first YB-60 reveals details of the swept-wings as well as the swept vertical tail and horizontal stabilizers and elevators. Not visible are retractable tail wheels to stabilize the rear of the plane during the first moments of takeoff. (San Diego Air and Space Museum)

Top left: Like the preceding photo, this view of the first YB-60 was taken during a visit to Edwards Air Force Base in January 1953. In the background is a late-model B-36. The access hatch is open between the "Convair" and "YB-60" below the cockpit. (National Museum of the United States Air Force) **Top right:** The tail wheels are lowered on YB-60 49-2676. It was extended during the takeoff run and was retracted just before rotation. During a landing, the tail wheel was not lowered until both the main wheels and the nose wheels were firmly touching the runway. **Above left:** The first YB-60 is viewed head-on. The streamlined nose with the nose probe contoured into its front gave this aircraft a much sleeker look than the B-36, with its rounded, almost blunt, nose. The second YB-60 had an even more pointed, streamlined nose. **Above right:** The second YB-60, serial number 49-2643, is under construction at Convair's Fort Worth plant. The nose section is lying on the floor in the foreground to the right of center. Both of the forward top turrets are mounted and are in the raised position, bay doors lowered

Although the B-36 and its reconnaissance-bomber version the RB-36 never dropped a bomb in anger, and although controversies swirled around it in the interservice disputes of the late 1940s and early 1950s, this aircraft served a valuable purpose as a deterrent to Soviet military ambitions and as a testing platform for a variety of new technologies. Only a handful of these Cold-War behemoths survive, including this one, B-36J-1-CF serial number 52-2220, on display at the Air Force Museum. (National Museum of the United States Air Force)